I Forgive You
JOURNEY TO RECOVERY

by Queen V

DORRANCE
PUBLISHING CO
EST. 1920
PITTSBURGH, PENNSYLVANIA 15238

Dorrance Publishing Co
585 Alpha Drive
Suite 103
Pittsburgh, PA 15238
Visit our website at *www.dorrancebookstore.com*

ISBN: 979-8-8860-4380-8
eISBN: 979-8-8860-4473-7

I Forgive You
JOURNEY TO RECOVERY

Contents

Acknowledgements

Thank you to Cesarina Sanchez, De'vaughn Person, and Shamah ShaRize for their contributions to this work. I also thank my focus team for their support, guidance, and gracious corrections throughout this process. Thank you all for your assistance to bring my dream to fruition.

You Get Me

Mind racing, heart beating out of my chest…how do you know me so well

I look in your eyes I see me looking back
We share intimate moments & could swear we are one…giving myself to you
is so easy…you get me

Lying in your arms, the world melts away
Listening to your heartbeat beneath my ear and I know you were made just for me
You say my name and my private spaces call for your touch…you get me

Conversations touching so many places in the universe is only one gift. You
take me on a ride, hanging on tight so not to miss a word or gesture. Wisdom
from on high spills from lips Perfection you do not proclaim however strive
for it you do…you so get me

Daily challenges plague you and you share them with a friend. Your concerns
& fears whisper to be tucked away on the pages of my heart with honor. Trust
& loyalty shield you & protect from the world. Honor & respect the weapons
used to take on countless foes. The mask in place when needed, but which one
do I wear now? Yeah, you get me

At my side you stand, ready for war at a moment's glance…fight, fight, we do
it all the time to see who loves the other more. You have blessed me in so many
ways, the cosmos may never know, but rest & always know you GOT ME from
the word go…cause you get ME!!!

Veils

Erected protection
Walls to guard me or protect you
Mystery in my eyes will draw you in
Cut your throat if you play games within

Stand behind a wall of secrets
Bodies rest before I fall
Danger in the darkness
No soldiers do I call

Wrestling with demons & angels too
Facing another battle
Not sure what to do
Bloody, scared yet going through

You think you know me
Through the dark places I have been
I'll wear the veils today
Hiding the pain, no misery
However at the end of the day I claim the victory
Tomorrow not promised to none
Today is my blessing
Says I already WON

WHERE DO I GO NEXT?

Where do I go next? I'm starting all over but I know for a fact that the world will not ever let me forget one mistake. My ridiculous, one absurd mistake that will always be a blot on my life. How will I ever lay it down? The mistake in my youth will haunt me to the day I die. Will I ever be able to move on to the next level? Choices made in haste once upon a blue moon should not be the standard by which others define me. The power to move from one situation to the next, has now erected a barrier which has and will forever alter my progress from this point forward. I'm tired of asking permission to live my life. Rehabilitation takes its pound of flesh. The Man. The Woman. At times, strips you of your humanity, & gives you a tan or green jumpsuit to cover your core until they strip you again. Whether it's mealtime or count, restricted calls that are monitored for my own safety. Violated mail and conversations. They want to make sure I'm not loved too much. Anyone that can anchor me, have been added to the list of resources out of my reach. How do I ask someone to stand with me through this mess… the missed kisses, the tender promises, our commitment never included any of this business. I have a hard time wrapping my brain around it myself. It happened so fast. One decision in the blink of an eye has altered my path and is leading me down a road that I don't think I was bargaining for. Making rent, buying grub for my table, putting shoes on my lil' man's feet…he didn't ask to be here. That's my job to cover him/her until they can do for themselves.

The stain on my Spirit has also influenced how I see myself. Was it the bracelets closing around my wrist, the constant exposure to the mood swings of the COs during search. The isolation from loved ones who have had enough of this journey that they did not choose? Or was it the violation of My personal space when I bend over & spread for the officer of the day. Even worse when it's a trustee who earned his/her bones on their knees? At least let me CHOOSE if I will give it up!!

Choices, implied freedoms, would I do it again the same way knowing what I know now? What it will cost me, my shorty, my relationships, my parents, the opportunity to say goodbye to someone who didn't sign up for this in the first place. That split-second decision now haunts me. I tell my story after the fact, it's a reference point. Say I meet someone new. Do I share the person I am now instead of the representative? I want to tell my secret but I know the embrace will be different. The perception of who I used to be has now changed. Let me find out!!!

The Iroquois Indians say, "you laugh when it has hit too close to home." Can they be comfortable with what they don't know, I'm not telling because I already see that you can't handle me. I was kidding myself to believe someone like you would be interested in someone like me; less than, not equal to. Sentence has been imposed, GUILTY of lying about who I am…not to be trusted. Indicted and sentenced to life. This mask is sooo HEAVY. I want to put it down but can't figure out who do I ask permission.

These lines will give you a peak into the journey of my redemption. Efforts to change take on many forms. The authors of these pages are sharing so they can erect a message. A warning some would say. "Don't travel the same road because it leads to destruction, despair, loss of focus and so much more that you can do without." It's hard to keep starting over & over again. However, on the other hand, as a blessing and a curse. Some of us have to walk our journey to learn it's relevant lessons. However, when the lesson is learned, share it. It begins the restitution to your soul for all lost. The liberation of your Spirit begins with YOU. YOU DESERVE IT. We deserve it. I CLAIM IT.

What do I do with this?

There is a feeling in my bosom that I can't explain. I have health & strength but nowhere to call my own… have skills & drive but no job to apply it to… what do I do with this?

The yearning to give life but no embrace or seed in my womb…what do I do with this?

I possess rags with tags and swivel in my hips that must be set free…what do I do with this?

A dream to change the future, not to mention even charisma to charm a snake…what do I do with this?

Doubt, envy, charity and loyalty also dwell in that same space…what do I do with this?

Instead of walking with head down and admitting confusion or defeat, I think I'll go back to the source and ask the question…what do I do with this?

However while there remember to say THANK YOU for all that I am and will be…What can the world do with ME???

Port in the storm

I open my eyes
turn my head to survey the room
haze starting to lift
the buzz from the last few... starting to lift
surroundings not familiar
not sure I care

reach for my phone
comfort anchor in any situation
blurry eyes focus
oh shit!!
where am I?
reality crashes in...
yesterday's fun & today's reality collide
fun exit stage left, enter adult...aww shit

where is my...?
need my keys…fuck!!
everything lands where it can
... and the day smacks the fuck out of me

yelling at staff
... don't want to check in with anyone
voice message from unfamiliar friend & pics..
wtf, slight grin as I review...shame wants to visit...I soooo needed this
not sure what is was & really don't care

who was that!!…teasing from my pal during smoke break brings me back.…
deep sigh...oooohhh yeah...smile reminds me
"'I needed that'

gobble down some nasty $1 pizza while darting to next meeting
look at desk, some more bullshit 'NOT MINE' up there...what day is it again?

When A Family Falls Apart

Sunday, Mornings
Family, Lounging
Mother, Solitaire
Father, Kitchen
Aunty, Watching the Kids
Kids, Watching the TV
Family, Peaceful

September, 2003
TV, The Preachers Wife
We, Watching
Laughing, Loving
Singing, Playing
Mother, Baby
Holding, Bonding
Moment, Tense
Mother, "Take the baby to Aunty, I feel lightheaded"
Me, Taking
Turning, Walking
Aunty, "LISA"
Me, Looking
Mommy, Shaking
Eyes, Rolling
Me, Freezing
Confused, Scared
Ambulance, Coming
Mommy, Leaving
Now This 10-Year-Old Boy Has No More,

Sunday, Mornings
Family, Lounging
Mother, Solitaire
Father, Kitchen
Aunty, Baby
Kids, Playing
We, Broken

SALUTE

For those of you who held down your seed on cheddar from a bullshit job
For those of you that got pushed out because the crazy "ONE" found a new stick
For those who would crawl across broken glass to see that little smile
For those who did it all alone and never said a word
For those who changed the diapers,
…that know two A.M. feedings & colic cry
…that went to parent teacher conferences & the class trips too
…that read bedtime stories & carpool…that's just what we do
…if you stood in for the donor
…if you bought sneakers & uniforms just to help out
…if you made the call each week when it's your turn to use the phone
…if you gave your name without DNA
…if you went to graduation & were the loudest there
…if you never get recognized,
YOU KNOW WHO YOU ARE…SALUTE…WE wouldn't be here without YOU

Trade offs

Want?
Desire?
Need?
Do I know the difference?
What does that look like?
How will I know?
What does it mean to you?
Want...desire...need
They are confused terms
Frustrating to those who may attempt to look within

Getting up
Grinding
Existing
Paying the bills
The light grows dimmer, but the grind goes until you win
Making it from day to day, holding on to dreams of what could, should be
Glimmers of what could be just out, out of reach
Carrot calling me to a greater end

Needs...basic issues that I Have to Have
Essentials my babies deserve, demand....
I look at them sleeping so sound trusting me
What do I tell them when I can't figure out the mystery
Why am I here...can I do this on my own?
No one can or will as I

No one gets it...NO ONE!!
Frustrations about what was, is, what should be, a barrier to my greed
Imprinted on my soul, success for my progeny
Hoping for strength & endurance to achieve
I look in the eyes of my treasures

They're trusting only me
It's in my head...who knows why I hear the call
My angels are a gift, I will protect with my life
A blessing I owe them...unclaimed check that I'm yet to sign
Why did He trust them to me, I'll never know
I can barely do me...come on where am I supposed to go?
 I need answers to questions never asked but I need this, THIS to face tomor-
row...miracle has to show up

Desire... dream just out of reach
How things are supposed to be,
 if I ever get a chance to make history
The Creator sent me to write my name in a place I've never seen
A victory for me to claim, some called destiny
He dared me to believe
Dreaming of a better day, a better way
Somehow I will find the key to the smiles, the joy, & peace that I have already
claimed
You see my heart's desire
 To let freedom reign
Dreams of a better day for me or mine
Conquering hatred, redefining creed
Raising the bar & touching eternity

WORTHY

Hey there little one, my beloved Angel

Do you know you are a precious from the Creator? If you didn't ever hear that before, I want to sit with me for a moment beloved and let me 'fill your cup.'

You were born to two silly teenagers in a little back water town in the 60s. That is significant because they didn't know their head from their ass and neither did anyone else. However, finances brought your mother to a dark place that she felt unloved. Her solution was to get involved with your father; a jock, dream catch of the town…working, handsome, lady's man that everyone wanted. Low & behold she caught his eye and his seed. Not knowing how to raise a family he ran rather than go to jail. Limited education raised his brothers & forever helping mother made him run from responsibility and commitment. Not knowing anything else, Mom followed behind her baby daddy.

Frustration & fear fed them for a long while until black eyes and hurtful words entered along with cops. Grandma jumped up and ran to Mom's side to save her life & yours…felt responsible for the actions of her seed.

You were conceived and nurtured…suckled on fear, poverty, anger, disappointment, and so much negativity that the saints had to look away. However, you need to hold on to the knowledge that you sprung forth from strong stock. You were blessed with armor around your heart and mind. Yes you will face some battles but remember it will not defeat you soldier. The warrior in you will not let you drop your head even when you drop to one knee.

Long story short, Grandma swooped in with her shield and spear to save the family that she helped create. She weaved a cocoon of love around her 'chicks' and prayed a covering of prosperity & protection over them…leaving nothing to chance. She not only taught hers the 'Art of War.' She equipped other princesses on how to fight their battles too. She planted seeds of hope, strength & faith…grounded in the Creator. She fed your Spirit with hugs & kisses, as well as with recipes & strategies of how to overcome…wisdom of the ancients imparted throughout time.

Then one day you came with a seed of your own and the same fear that grandma had seen so often in the past, now stood before this Queen yet again attempting to conquer one more. Beloved, remember how you used to sit & play in your Queen's hair, her crown. Sat at her side to hear the family pearls of wisdom, listen to the recipes of how to cook a meal & hold a family together. Beloved, did you realize you are a precious flower that she prayed for and watered with love? She called you her daughter because she could never have a girl. It was as if her kids blessed her with you, a special treasure that was called you. The acceptance, unconditional love, peace, joy, satisfaction, spirit of the warrior…that you have, spilled off her saucer. Running over for all to partake. Your Queen imparted a portion of her strength. She then went on to claim her crown…job well done; words so profound.

Beloved, you a mighty jewel in the crown of the King. You are fearfully and wonderfully made. You were stitched together, dare say, crafted, for such a time as this. It is hard to comprehend at times that pain is necessary. However, the Bad Bitch you are destined to become will be crafted by the hands of controversy and confusion. You will find your way through the madness because you are a weapon forged in the furnace of struggle. Destiny knows your name. Glory knows every tear you have and will ever shed. Time knows your end from the beginning. Your journey is moving on ahead.

Beloved, no one can fix all those dark spaces that were never addressed. All it can do is offer an apology for the times you had to face struggle alone. For the time you did not get what everyone else had… guidance, protection, safety, honor, respect, charity. Don't really understand how you're still standing sometimes. The beating your Spirit has taken over the years astounds, almost mesmerizes at times but look what it has yielded, a beautiful, charming, intelligent, humble, articulate…soldier that can conquer any battlefield she puts her mind to. Do understand, little one, you have a mission, to leave this world a little better than when you got here. Although do hear this, your presence has made a difference…in places you may never know…it's yet to be revealed. This piece of wisdom I impart now, BE THE BEST YOU EACH DAY, please…an awesome gift…warrior for all time…loaded, cocked, & ready for the war of a lifetime.

Still strangers

Well here I am writing you again
And I know you are like...again?
Bcuz you didn't receive the first two letters
which had too much truth
and truth is not accepted in a world full of lies
bcuz lies heal the tormenting reality that truth brings
so I continue to lie to you in order to not hurt you…in order to not deceive you…
so our relationship will be built on dishonesty and we will never know each other
You will never know the change
bcuz the change is always changing
so I will never know the me
and you will never know the we
and we will forever be what we are right now
Still Strangers

Thank you

Acknowledged in the hearts of those yet to be born
Your shoulders carried a load that you never knew was yours
Graced every day to rise and be a blessing called YOU

I called you my Queen because you taught me to walk with grace and poise...funny never knew that's what you did

Command of your domain never questioned by those around
Awesome beauty and talent...oh how proud

Smiles and joy from your love I always knew
Bandaged my hurts with cupcakes and cartoons
Walked beside me in those crazy days and helped me to weather the storms
Lady, how I miss your funny lil' poems & songs

Love abounding from the dishes for the family
History, music & the Ancestors you shared with me
Patience of a saint & voice of an angel that forever will echo in the chambers of my heart

Absent is presence means you stand with the King
He lent you to me to water my spirit, fertilize my dreams and comfort my dark days

I can't say goodbye to you because I still feel you walking with me.
Your wisdom guided my steps and your guarded me from hidden pitfalls that you already travailed
Lady you are so awesome...power in this life and in the next...do you see what you did.
That little girl that was scared, hurt, battered and abused back in the dark woods of Georgia
Carried horror in her bosom to places that she never imagined she would ever see herself
The ripple you started so many moons ago has traveled and conquered shores that are credited to you
So here today I bless you with your flowers that will never be enough for all you gave to me

Salute...My Queen...thank you

My lil' man

I have such high hopes for you
The dreams & wishes, how do I help them come true?

Your smile lights my day
Helps me grin and get through,
 the challenges I see erected before you
Taking your first steps into destiny
Instilling tales of glory...of those before you
The first black cop, lawyer, judge in our town...some would hope say first
black...no I can't, cuz I want...

Defeating statistics
Born loser what you were deemed
Dodging bullets, daggers...there were more than a few
Compliments on your stature and physique flowed like a stream

They said look at your ears and it will tell where he will go
I reached down inside me to grab seeds ready to share, with prayers for you to grow

Geography, history, English too
Tools for others...just not for you
You carved a different path that no one had blazed
The hurt and confusion I saw, had me crazed
A check he wrote yet could not cash until payday
Robbing Peter to pay Paul, we made our way

The streets & other factors too called you names I
 pray you'll never know
A better world I want for you though...as we watch your son now blaze a trail
of a star burning bright

Wondering where your father was
A lil' man lost in his own fantasy...yeah?

Reality hit him but he didn't understand
The challenges he & I were facing shouldn't have stood between him and his
lil' man

You stand there strong and tall
Your lil' one at your side
Looking at who he could become with pride
A soldier, pilot, fireman...all heroes in my eyes for now
However, one day he will see what a great awesome fabulous, intelligent, hand-
some, terrific man ...mother's love sees the battles we conquered...watching
your greatness build

My lil' man, I stand and witness the feats you perform
To think the cocktail of love from many moons ago, tuned into the blessing
called you

Not My Job

Duck. Swing. Jab.
Uppercut
Duck, ah damn it Run!!!

Pack your shit
Let's go
I'm ready when you are

What?
You're staying…for how long?
Is IT that good? Is it worth your life?
I'll give you that one..!!
But know this…
You got one more time for me to see that…!!

Come on!!!
Please can we leave? I can't stand to see u like this…Remember I got you!!!

Again??…what happened this time…
You know what…really don't care to hear it again.

We can't stay…we gotta go…
I gotta go…I can't do this any more

There is so much I want to tell you but I can't… this has been going long enough.
I love you and always will BUT…THIS, This right here…I can't do this anymore

Where were you?
I needed you and you weren't there
I called out but no one answered
I was there for you but you left me out there all alone
You were supposed to…

You stay if you want to
I have to go
…before one of us stops breathing
I will always be there when you call however that was never my job

Thank you for teaching me to stand tall through it all.
Thank you for limiting the scars
Some you will never see…I thank you for that too.
I thank you for all you gave me
However it's my job to take care of me now

PRAISES

I just want to scream
Won't wake up until my skin breaks
Bleeding new blessings
From old lessons to those yet to come
My mind hurts
& I was done with love
But this bitch shadowed eternity
Now I'm done…need some hugs
Contradiction walking
I breed the grudge

Going apeshit to prove who I am
Knights don't know themselves; let alone me
Need the pain of success
Tired of ordinary
Prosperity, I claim. But bodies will have to Fa too
The battle is real…not going down alone

Failure Is Not an Option

Steadily poppin
Face in a book
History repeats
So I'm hip when the bodies droppin
Hurt in my soul
Continue 2 stroll
Continue to grow

Growth beyond your measure
Your greedy but deserve the glow
My heart heard the lie
Joy is all you saw
Chase it…it belongs to you
I want it
I'm gonna catch it
Mine. Mine. MINE???
Need to claim my joy…one minute, two, three
I need to know…peace, happiness, love!!!

Love u different when the pen strokes
Taste ur thoughts
U stood on line 4 me
Square shoulders & thick heads

Taught me how to spit a rhyme
Life on the line for me
Sip the wine 4 me
Dared me to diss u
Underwent patdowns
Pride smacked down
True Soldier
Never seen u back down

Never seen u frown
That crown, you wear it well
Walked tall when others fell

Changed my world in many ways
Simple encouragement given on many a day
Standing in the shadows you lifted my wings
I take these words & lines to give back a myriad of blessings
Thank you, Universe, for this special gift
Honor & Praises I MUST lift!!

MASKS

Masks mounted and shed every day
Roles assumed seep into being
Push back to find the balance yet conquer its space
Standing tall in reverence to the majesty that is me
Defending the world I hold dear
Motivation in one light
Terror in another
Representatives come to give what they know
Slight issue, script change, setting out of sync
Character flaw exposed by slip of the tongue
Treasures left unguarded while we save the world
Selfish or Selfless...not sure of which
Answers I reach for in conversation with faith
Purpose or mistake?
Journey/destiny or Colossal failure?
Preparation or Crisis...I, I, I DETERMINE which
Creator, Ancestors, that which holds ME TOGETHER I implore you, don't give up. We are still above dirt...so grateful for another day...another chance, another opportunity to pull down the mask to see Me
Clear your mind and let's get ready for.....

FIX YOUR FACE

Tuck it away
Nobody wants to see it
They really could care less
Got enough drama of their own
Gotta handle s***
Fix your face

I'm not gonna tell you again…!!!
What happens in my house stays in my –
Go wash your face & get it together
If you don't, I will
Fix your face

I ain't did nothing to you yet
I don't wanna see that
You know what you did to piss me off
So help me, if you embarrass me I …
Go fix your face

I bust my ass to make sure your good
You really wanna start this
You ain't seen nothing yet
Go fix your face

I wear a mask to hide the shame, guilt, & disgrace…all too familiar friends
Seems like I can never do anything right
If this keeps up, I don't know what
(Looking at the black eye & bruise on my face)…can't stand the marks every-
where else
I guess I betta
Go fix my face

Carnal knowledge

tonight will go down in history

you touched me in ways that will leave impressions on secret places that a lady never talks about

today I have to break that tradition

you slipped ur fingers around my xxxx and in & out so many times and made me...ahh

can I truly say things like that out loud or in my diary

written on butterfly wings or some would say those bats flying in my belfry

you actually let him do that to you!!

he put his foot where?

behind my head gurl

no he didn't...no I did not think my body could do that

the freak came out and I had to put her back

if I want some more…

as I said ladies don't talk about stuff like that

gurl I had to tell someone

...looked back in the mirror as I was preparing my next answer...it was so good, it had me talking to myself

Marking Time

Today begins again
not knowing where it is taking me
mysteries unfold
I answer the query

drama of the past ...haunts me
asking if this is the way, the way I'm supposed be?
decisions made in haste changed my world
staying the course to get to my purpose
I need to see where this road will lead

time tells me keep moving before I get You
lovers, family, friends...pass you by sharing space during a conversation or a
moment becoming a memory
I need to see if the pain will ever make a difference to anyone but ME
did I answer the question I see, hear in me?
there is a hurt in me NO ONE can answer for
BUT I NNNEEEEEEDDD SOMEONE TOO!!!

you hurt me and walked away...thank you
Your loss
a precious jewel that you will never see shine
I reach for the stars to ascend to my throne
stationed to watch the next generation OUTDO Me
helping hands is what I received and will bless the next
standing in pathway of time
aided by queens & kings who watch from glorious places
make you proud is all I ever wanted to do
however now I stand tall to say thank you for all you did
I'm here today because of grace
although the gift I leave is as they say...
PRICELESS
Thank you Creator for each and every day
marking time is not what I do

reaching on to see if the coast is clear…shady doctors & pallbearers seem to
chase my shadow

Nothing important

630 is my deaf sentence knowing I made it throw another night feeds my depression the very life I wish to end

Fighting every image that plays like reruns in my heart, my eyes being the screen to my everlasting torture

My day begins with the slow screams of what if and graduates to now a smile and be tortured in silence

Throughout the day I sit in defeat knowing that depression and anxiety will always be the fights I can't win

Wishing that I was a better mother to my beautiful spirit of a child, knowing one day he will see me for who I truly am, hoping he will still love me broken, never being the mother he wanted but just an image of what if

Beating myself to be the woman that he once loved, knowing that can never be, cause that woman died loving him. Seeing him as he is a father she wishes she had and as the husband she dreamed of as a young child

Nighttime comes and I fight to sleep dreaming of emptiness, never truly sleeping just lying there hoping I would never wake again

Dear Dear Friend

Dear Dear Friend…why did you leave so soon?
Wisdom…Before and beyond your time
You dropped it like grapes on the vine
There for the picking or stepping if one had the courage
The pleasure and honor was mine
You called my thoughts higher
Perceptions never to be the same
Sage one, why did you leave me all alone?
Looked over my shoulder, you beamed tall and proud
I turned away for a moment…still don't understand why you couldn't stay
I needed you to walk with me for a few more strides
You told me, 'You know the way'
I never got a chance to tell you how much you meant to me …
 How you changed my world
An angel whispered, 'my job is done, the crown you want, she already earned'

'beloved I didn't abandon you…my time has come to claim my peace.
I came to comfort you and say farewell. Whisper my name and I will tell the
angels to say hello…dear friend we will never say goodbye'
I think of that promise and know that when my day comes I will also be able
to share that precious moment, a precious gift to release a Dear Dear Friend

Sleep in Power & Peace

Ladies Roll Call
Ladies, when I call your name, I want you to step up and give the other sisters in the room a pearl of wisdom from your corner of the world

Mother?
Here...my children are a major part of my world. They are a better part of me that calls up the strength, life lessons and endurance to take care of and guide my precious treasures to their rightful place

Daughter?
Here...I'm the one Daddy protected when he was home. I'm also the one Mommy relied on and shared secrets with. Gifts given, not sure what they are for…but I'm here

Wife?
Here...partner to a great man that sees the world in a unique way. He loves me when the rest of the world turns it's back. Not always sure he knows how to show his love sometimes; different lens to look through. He sees things in me that have never been appreciated before

Student?
Here...experiencing the universe to see where I fit in. Formal & informal lessons shape my thoughts of me. Looking for my purpose. Want to know how I can make this world, my corner of it, better than when I got here

Artist?
Here...I want to share the blessing of being alive in a different way; to call forth the healing inside all of us. If we take some time to listen to the Creator, the creation planted inside us will bless those around us

Entrepreneur?
Here...I apologize for being disrespectful to the status quo. Maybe I shouldn't. I need to show the world a better way of doing things and make some money

to take care of my community. I have learned the flaws in the other financial systems and I'm willing to take a chance on me. I don't like authority, especially when you can't explain to me why your ways you're capitalism are hurting people is pain necessary to make a dollar

Healer?
Here...I have the patience and stamina to walk through humanity to shoulder some of the burdens that were distributed unfairly. I take on wounds to help your gift come through. I'm nothing special. My job is to support your climb to your place of honor if you want it. I'm here to witness your struggle and say you matter until you can say it to yourself

Ladies...for those of you who didn't want to speak up tonight, please shine your light. Let the world know you are an essential part of this mess. You may have the solutions of the world's crisis in your Spirit. Our existence will never be the same without your presence... Salute

HOW DO I TELL YOU?

I lost something that means so much to me…please could you help me find it? A little while back I put it over here & now it's not there. I have been looking for it for a minute but I still can't find it…could you help me please???

Thank you so much for your time but I can't even tell you the last time I saw it. A precious person in my life purchased it for me, just cause…I NEED TO FIND IT!! I need to find it. I don't know what I would do if I couldn't find it. I have lost sooo much…I can't lose this too. Please, please can you help me? I don't have much…could you please help me???

It's this one right here!!! Can't take your eyes off it. Can you watch it for me please…can you? It lights a room. It can lead you to anything you are looking for.

Why did you say that? What part of this are you not getting? You can't hurt me any more than I have already hurt myself. I hate myself more than you will ever know. I probably allowed dumb shit into my world that no one could or should have.

But thank you.
You gave me a life lesson
Moreover, I didn't lose my life or anything important
Damn sure not you. I shed the best 150+ pounds {in amazement I step back & review the site}… of not what I lost but at the glow over what I gained

Overdue conversation
Don't like yesterday
Tomorrow is filled with fear
Rejection seen at every touch

You can't give me what u don't know
How do I ask for something of u if I don't even know I want it?

Tears well up in a place that is overcrowded with drama that ur mama don't really want
How do I address a problem that no one knows how to find the solution?

You know you in ur dark place! But how can u tell me who I'm supposed to be...while standing next to you?

Mommy...Daddy? what happened?
Why did u do this to me? were u even thinking of me in the back of...

Time doesn't respect anyone that looks like me...quiet as it's kept
Passing is a lie that we tell ourselves to sleep at night. Yeah, we pray that it is true...or do we?
Passing by, passing through, getting over bcuz no one can tell who u supposed to be

Talking to myself to quiet the spirit just beneath the skin.
Beating {heart} me...rhythm in my head...so out of time, pace not letting catch up...yet telling me who I AM??
I listen for the the answer to questions that no one wants to ask...treasuring a pay day that no one is willing to ante up for

I'm here why?
I'm still here why?
Why am I asking you this shit? You don't know, u don't have the power, wisdom or authority to respond...shut the fuck up...u don't have enough money or time to pay for the privilege of my company

Woo...take a breath...listen to that beat, the power in your breast...dance to your drummer, write your own song...whispers to my spirit while watching my lil' angel sleep so tenderly

A moment, a year, a lifetime in those lil' hands, that precious smile, first steps into destiny.
Little one, my dream, my tomorrow...not sure who I was meant to be, however the twinkle in your eye gives me strength to carry on. Little angel sent through time to bless me. Thank you for the chance to be your...

How do U/I...?

how do u explain to someone who doesn't know u that your partner just left u a few weeks ago with the rent due, no solid childcare, no family support that u want (?) to speak of...the smile of your bundle of joy, that lights up your world with a fall or a new feat, that they don't matter to the other parent after striving soooo hard?

how do u explain to ur partner that your boss is riding your ass for everything, you can't find the money to pay the rent and/or put food on the table...how do u explain to ur partner that I sooo appreciate u making me that same bologna sandwich for the eighth time at 2 A.M. while the baby is teething and I can't afford to buy meds to quiet him down or afford doctor bills or pampers when I begged them to agree to the birth?

how do u explain going to your fourth interview in one day, not being so perky bcuz I need a job, any job so my kid can eat pizza instead of ramen noodles!...how do you reach out to a case manager who u see when times are bad...who doesn't listen to u when u want to report that u got that minimum wage job on part time hours, who gave you a song and dance down at HRA bcuz u have to fight for your food stamps after the job gave u 25 cent raise on a job u don't want but can't afford to quit?

how do u wake up every morning and look at a partner that u want to tell to leave, hit the curb...that if u could bash their head in & hide the bloody dismembered body in a hole somewhere to suffer and rot they would be there already...how do u explain to that stupid bastard you laid next to the funds, that u were more scared of telling ur partner than thinking, fearing them...losing my life or looosssssiiinnnnggg my life...do u get it? life in hell or eternal purgatory?

how do u explain to ur next that ur ex hurt u sooo bad that ur heart is in a place that u can't find bcuz exposing it to anyone would hurt everybody? how do u explain to that special partner that if I hear ur voice b4 I shake off the outside world I will choke the life out of u as if u were that supervisor who's just doing their job to tell u get off the property...thank you, COVID!! company gone & so am I?

how do u explain to ur mental health professionals that u want to demolish all traces of the company u worked for, missed ur kid's special moments for... chose them over significant other moments, gave them every ounce of yourself to keep food on the table...how do u explain that?

how do u explain that u have no energy but to fall asleep in the presence of ur loved one saying thank you for being here...all they tend to see is a lazy prick not interested in their happiness...how do u explain that u NEED the touch, the comfort, the smile of ur loved one and all of the rest of the world & its ugliness, abuse, & horror fall away?...how do u explain that WE exist bcuz it puts a smile on MY face, even of it's for a moment, hour, day, week...u live here to make ME happy for a while, bcuz that brings ME an ounce of joy...how do I explain that...will I ever understand what I'M willing to give to get a few memories of happy...how do u explain they bring ME joy and help ME go on each day, each challenge, each trauma...how do u help someone understand they r part of ur peace and I'M soooo grateful to have them in MY world...how do I explain...? {it to me}

Mis-d

Misunderstood...love & mercy offered and abused

Misguided...wrong agenda being pushed toward progress

Misled...involved in a situation that had nothing to do with me

Mistake...resources engaged in war not mine

Misdirected...energy given freely under false pretenses

Misrepresented...never meant to give me what you promised

Misspoke...thought you said you loved me

Mislabeled...you never thought I could be an asset

Misalliance...you never saw the challenge coming but not willing to give in, admit you didn't see all the moves in play

Misgiving - your Spirit picking up something that doesn't seem to have a credible explanation

Mistrust - ugliness touched my Spirit and struggling to find my way back to me

Misinterpret - representatives not able to be themselves for fear of abandonment

Misapprehend- can't understand what is your drama if we don't know each other

Misjudge...review of facts not adding up

Misconstrue...alter facts to suit own perception

Miscreant - you are breaking laws in my world to preserve the ones in yours

Miseducation - love map, love language, love choices, new trauma mistakenly built into growth & development

High Anxiety

WTF
I hear this Bullxxxx
Making me grind my teeth through my jaw
It rings in my ears
My spirit on high alert
What's going on?
Drama drama everywhere
Nerves on edge
Can't decide my next step
Today Tomorrow all a fluid blur
Gun on hip Cocked & ready

Bills, doctors, diapers, food
Situation out of control
No comfort in familiar arms
Not a word can ease troubled soul

One more word, I will crack his jaw
Sleep offers no comfort
Sippie not strong enough
Trees, a forest…the haze can't hide the pain

Prayer a gift from above
Not bright enough to sit still
Damn my spirit is so needy
Need some attention, need answers
Need to unload my brain & not pick it back up!
Distant memories show strength that no one knows how to tap into

Miserable
Want to give up & give in
Oh Hell NO!!
Made of true grit

Standing on the shoulders of great ones
Failure not an option
Victory already mine
Strap up
Dig in
War until one falls & moves no more
Fears flow like rain but never stop the arrow from its destination…destruction
to hypocrisy & ridicule…my shield has shifted but never fell. It guards the
heart & soul of the warrior preparing for battle.

I'll take this day and tomorrow too
I claim this victory & so much more
My destiny & my course are mine to command
The time has come for me to claim ALL THAT I AM!!!!!

I want to hate you

U came into my world and changed my point of view
U made me feel so good that I looked at me differently.
I liked who I saw in your eyes
The new me walked taller, stood for something, took on challenges that I never
would have tackled except for the fact that I had u on my side
The rest of the troops fell away because all they saw was U...the person U
helped Me become

Flag on the play...new players in the game
That light that used to shine for me has now turned to another.
When did I lose favor, I didn't see it coming
I wish I could, oh how I want to so bad...to Hate U

Days gone by... I never realized the strategy of our movement doesn't feel the same.
I heard you say my name and your tone doesn't ring in my ear or my heart the same
U tried to explain, 'I didnt mean it to turn out this ...' the lies are the same but
I hear them for what they R now
I wish I could, oh how I want so bad... to Hate U

The smile I carried in my heart changed to a familiar look that I didn't realize
I missed.
A comfortable friend that I knew very well
Carried my shield so all could tell
I put it down when I noticed the bird flying over was not a buzzard yet an
angel sent to help me heal.

I can't , actually, will never be able to hate you
During good, bad, or shady times you taught me to stand my ground for Me.
I can't hate the new Me
Standing in victory
I wish I, oh how I want to so bad...to HATE U
I LOOK AROUND
I look around and see hardship & struggle. He says to me you are my Queen
and never have to worry about that.

His broad shoulders and bigger heart carry his world and MINE. He lifts my barriers and covers my flaws. His calluses give me comfort just to know they are softened by my tears. I see him, hear his heart when he opens his mouth. His fear & anxiety are shrouded in courage & integrity. His dreams could change the world if he were ever given the power his titles truly command; Daddy, Lover, Friend, Husband, Champion, Soldier, Commander, Son, Father…

How could I miss something that I never knew I wanted. He's blessed me to see parts of world that no one has ever acknowledged before. He says it & then makes it so. I am proud of my journey at his side because it prepared me to be the woman, person that I am today. Happily, I carry the part of the load that he faulters under. He shrinks back and I am engaged. Activated without question. Reviewing the results, I see that it was a mission that was mine all along. My angel graced my life to reveal the power planted inside. My brief time at his side will live on in history because it created a new creature who now marches on to share that strength as a testimony to who we were.

Honor your loved ones with deeds to make them proud. A kind word every now and then makes the journey a little easier at times too.